D1378573

The World of Nature

AFRICAN PLAINS

GALLERY BOOKS
An Imprint of W. H. Smith Publishers Inc.
112 Madison Avenue
New York City 10016

This edition first published in U.S.
in 1991 by Gallery Books,
an imprint of W.H. Smith Publishers, Inc.
112 Madison Avenue, New York, New York 10016

ISBN 0-8317-9593-X

Printed and bound in Spain

For rights information about the photographs in
this book please contact:

The Image Bank
111 Fifth Avenue, New York, NY 10003

Producer: Solomon M. Skolnick
Writer: Alan Heatwole
Design Concept: Lesley Ehlers
Designer: Ann-Louise Lipman
Editor: Sara Colacurto
Production: Valerie Zars
Photo Researcher: Edward Douglas
Assistant Photo Researcher: Robert V. Hale
Editorial Assistant: Carol Raguso

179888

Title page: The rainy season turns the African plains from a uniform gray to a lush green in a matter of weeks. Food and water become plentiful for the many grazing herds and the predators that feed upon them. *Opposite:* Kilimanjaro, an ancient volcano, remains the highest point on the African continent at 19,340 feet. It makes a majestic backdrop to the seemingly endless plains.

The short rainy season had started two weeks ago. In that brief period, the typically gray terrain was turned into a lush, exotic green, boasting a richness of life. Plants that had subsisted on scant rainfall under a searing-hot sun now flourished amidst heavy rains, flooded streams, and renewed lakes. New growth shot forth; trees were covered with leaves and blossoms; insects multiplied in the ponds and tall, rich grasses. Migratory birds, having returned from far-off lands, built new nests and fed on the abundant insects. The air came alive with their calling and singing and the fragrance of flowers and blossoms.

The vast, open plains of Africa teem with unique and luxuriant wildlife. Herds of large plant-eating mammals – several among the largest herbivores in the world – are accompanied by a myriad of predators and scavengers. The fastest, the tallest, and the largest land animals all share the African plains.

The savanna and bush land that intertwine to make up the African plains undergo a rapid and radical change during the wet season, for the climate is generally hot and very dry. To conserve water in the dry season, some plants have bulbs and tubers for underground water storage. Others store water in swollen stems or waxy leaves. Still other plants rely on deep root systems to tap underground water during long dry spells.

African lions, *Panthera leo,* rest on rocks in the Serengeti. Well-fed lions rest up to 20 hours a day; they hunt during early morning and evening.

Left: A full-grown male lion enjoys a light midday rain. *Below:* A lion's roar communicates his territory. The lion's mane, found only on adult males, protects them when sparring with other lions. *Opposite:* A young lion cub and its mother gaze out over the flat terrain. Cubs spend their first few months with their mother, away from the pride. Upon joining the pride, cubs quickly learn the hierarchy—males eat first, then cubs and females. *Following pages:* Lions are very social animals. When these cubs are older, the entire pride will share in the duty of rearing them.

Preceding page, above: The caracal, *Lynx caracal,* left, has black tufted ears, green eyes, and a soft tawny coat, which give this cat its unique beauty. The serval, *Felis serval,* right, resembles a small cheetah and likes to stalk birds, small rodents, and occasionally a small antelope in the tall grasses of the savanna. *Below:* Hunters kill servals for their fur, frequently passing the pelts off as cheetah. *This page, right:* The barely discernable spots of this black panther form the same pattern as those of other leopards—its blackness is merely a mutation. *Below:* In some areas of central and east Africa, the leopard, *Panthera pardus,* remains locally abundant, but the highly adaptable cat has become extinct in much of its former range, which included all of Africa as well as the Near and Middle East.

The only large tree truly suited to life on the plains is the gray baobab. It looks as though its roots are growing above ground; actually these are branches. The baobab's branches spread over a wide area, and where they touch down, the tree grows new roots, thus allowing it to spread over an expansive area.

Animals, as well, have become specialized to cope with the rigors of bush life. For the most part, mammals of the plains avoid direct competition with one another. Dik-diks eat only the bottom leaves of trees, while giraffes feed at the tops of trees. Similar animals often prefer different habitats: Elands usually traverse rocky hillsides; bongos wander through wooded areas; others, like impalas, prefer flat land.

The diversity found among the hoofed stock of Africa is unparalleled throughout the world. Antelopes, including the impala, gazelle, gnu, eland, topi, and kudu, add color to the plains as they feed on the grassland or browse the trees of the woodlands. The impala, Thomson's gazelle, and topi roam the grassland in large herds; generally antelopes that feed in the open congregate in great numbers because of the space and safety in numbers. Conversely, browsing antelopes such as the bongo and kudu live in smaller groups or even pairs. The trees of their forest habitat prohibit traveling in large formations while simultaneously serving as protection from predators.

A dozen distinct gazelle species inhabit the plains. They vary in size, color, shape of horns, and habitat. Due to this diversity and specialization, the gazelle is common throughout the entire continent of Africa, including the deserts.

Wildebeests, or gnus, form the largest herds of any of the hoofed stock. They are constantly on the move, migrating in the direction of rain, which they are able to detect up to 25 miles away. They rarely stop grazing except to sleep.

These pages: Leopards live in solitude. Spending most of their days in trees, they use the cover of the nighttime forest to ambush prey. Leopards show great strength and agility, climbing trees carrying prey that is sometimes heavier than themselves. *Following pages, left:* Despite its similarity to the leopard in size and coloring, the cheetah, *Acinonyx jubatus,* has different features, such as a small, round head and teardrop markings on its face. *Right:* Cheetahs prefer the light of day for hunting.

Preceding page: Cheetahs hunt in pairs, usually in the early morning or late afternoon and prefer fresh meat that they have killed themselves. Rarely will they eat carrion, especially from kills other than their own. *Below:* The cheetah's heavy tail helps the fleet feline maintain balance during high-speed turns. Cheetahs can attain speeds up to 75 mph but, in a chase, become exhausted after several hundred yards.

Hartebeests graze in much smaller groups – 10 to 20 animals. A smaller group, however, means a greater vulnerability to predators. To compensate for this, one hartebeest will alertly stand guard while the others eat. At the first sign of danger, it warns the others and the group is off, leaping into the air (pronking) as they run. As with most social, grazing mammals, the female hartebeests form groups with the calves; the males live in bachelor groups.

Flat and boundless, the plains imposes no size or territory restriction on its inhabitants. The largest and tallest animals alive today frequent the same grazing areas. Their size seems a successful adaptation to counter ferocious predators: adult hippopotamuses, rhinoceroses, elephants, and giraffes have no natural enemies aside from humans.

Hippopotamuses do little other than minimal grooming of one another during daylight hours. They spend the day floating in rivers or lakes, slowly digesting the quantities of food eaten the night before. Hippos rarely feed on aquatic vegetation; the bulk of their diet – grasses and fallen fruit – comes from dry land.

This page, top to bottom: **The nocturnal black-backed jackal,** *Thos mesomelos,* **is primarily a scavenger, although it is known to hunt birds, reptiles, and even immature gazelles. Dwarf mongooses,** *Helogale parvula,* **often occupy old termite hills and forage for insects, lizards, and eggs during the day. The African, or Cape, hunting dog,** *Lycaon pictus* **(pups are pictured) hunts in large packs and relentlessly pursues animals much larger than itself.** *Opposite:* **Spotted, or laughing, hyenas,** *Crocuta crocuta,* **usually hunt in packs at night. They have very strong jaws and, working as a team, easily kill such large prey as the zebra.**

Below: The wart hog, *Phacochoerus aethiopicus,* its face adorned with large knobs and tusks, feeds on short grasses during the day. At night it returns to its burrow, entering tailfirst so as to protect its hindquarters while it sleeps. *Opposite:* What's so funny? A spotted (laughing) hyena nurses her young. Spotted hyenas are much more aggressive than striped hyenas (*Hyaena hyaena*), which travel alone or in pairs and typically scavenge for food by night.

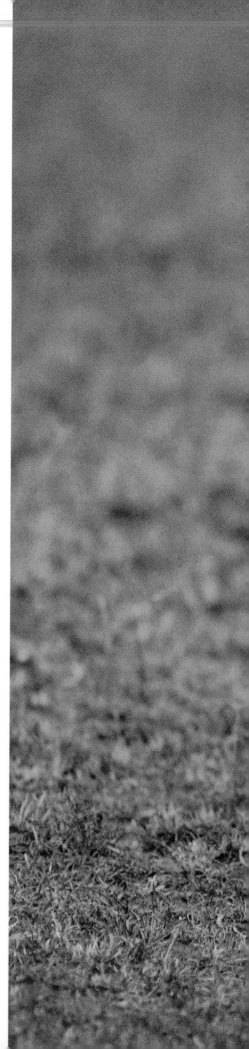

Above: Two African oryx, *Oryx gazella,* lock horns in a territorial dispute. Oryx, like several other antelopes, get moisture from plants and can survive for months without water. *Opposite:* The Defassa waterbuck, *Kobus ellipsiprymnus,* rarely strays far from water. It often plunges into deep pools to avoid approaching lions or wild dogs.

Above: A greater kudu, *Tragelaphus strepsiceros,* left, stands attentively in the grasslands of South Africa, where it feeds on grasses and fruit. Two male springboks, *Antidorcus marsupialis,* right, square off to determine dominance. Dutch settlers in southern Africa gave the springbok its name because of the animal's frequent leaping, which signals danger to others in the herd. *Below:* Topis, *Damaliscus lunatus,* typically stand on termite mounds to serve as sentries for the rest of the group. These beautiful antelopes have distinctive blue patches on their shoulders and haunches.

The night sees hippos come to life. They wade ashore and walk over well-traveled routes to grazing areas. These huge grass-eating machines busy themselves for hours feeding nonstop.

Hippos congregate in large herds. The females and calves mingle in larger groups – from 20 to 70 head – than do the males, which live apart from the females; males usually make their homes in inland mud wallows.

Without a doubt hippos belong in water. They swim aptly, or, as their water environment is often shallow, they simply walk over the bottom. They grow very little hair, but exude a pink mucous which lubricates their skin and protects it from the water. The ability to close their nostrils and ears also points to an aquatic life: Hippos can remain submerged for up to six minutes.

Unlike hippos, rhinoceroses feed during the day. There are two kinds of rhinos – the black and the white – but they differ in only a few ways. The basic body types of the two parallel one another, although the white rhino is larger than its black cousin; both have the familiar two horns on the snout and similar habits.

This page, top to bottom: **The Thomson's gazelle,** *Gazella thomsoni,* **one of the smallest of the true gazelles, roams grasslands in huge herds, which accounts for the leopard's predilection for them. The Grant's gazelle,** *Gazella granti,* **grows slightly larger than the Thomson's gazelle and is also favored food by cheetahs and leopards. A steenbok,** *Raphicerus campestris,* **browses on leaves at the edge of a forest, but will dash into the cover of the trees at the first sign of danger.** *Overleaf:* **To survive among the many large predators of the plains, the impala,** *Aepyceros melampus,* **has evolved leg muscles that enable it to leap 35 feet in a single bound.**

Preceding pages: Wildebeests, *Conno-chaetestaurinus,* travel in herds numbering more than 100,000. Their range extends from the southern portion of Africa's Serengeti to the northwest, where food and water is abundant at the start of the dry season. *This page, left:* A wildebeest charges across the grasslands of Serengeti National Park. Wildebeests can detect rainfall as far as 25 miles away. *Below:* A pair of wildebeests eats grass on the expansive plains of Kenya. These large grazers, also called gnus, rarely stop feeding except to sleep.

The white rhino is not actually white and the black rhino is not quite black. Rather the skin of the black rhino is a darker shade of gray than that of the white rhino. However, in both cases they more often take on the appearance of the mud in which they wallow.

Mud wallowing, common behavior among many large African mammals, serves several important functions. Wet mud conditions the animals' hides and cools them down. Also, mammoth beasts have more of a problem with tiny insects than with large predators. These giants rarely have an appendage with enough dexterity to remove small insects; even the elephant with its nimble trunk, cannot reach parts of its own body. Hence, many large mammals wallow in mud or dirt to rub off ticks, and the mud that sticks to their skin protects them from biting flies.

In a mutually beneficial relationship, tickbirds and cattle egrets frequent rhino grazing areas. Rhinos welcome the birds, which, perched atop the animals, feed on ticks and other parasitic insects. Aside from ridding rhinoceroses of parasites, the birds take off at any sign of danger, thus alerting rhinos to be on guard.

Weighing in at three to four tons, the rhinoceros and the hippopotamus rate as two of the world's largest animals. The African elephant, however, can grow to six tons, making it

Above: A Cape buffalo, *Syncerus caffer,* drinks from a stream in Kenya with an oxpecker, or tick bird, *Buphagus africanus,* perched on its horns. Buffaloes welcome these small birds, as they eat annoying insects and alert the huge beasts of danger by chirping and flying off. *Right:* Several Cape buffaloes rest in tall grass. Buffaloes seldom stray far from a river or watering hole. They feed during the night and early morning, after which they customarily rest or wallow in a mud hole.

A Burchell's zebra, *Equus burchelli*, neighs as it huddle with others in the Masai Mara National Reserve. Zebras eat tall grasses too tough for most other grazers. *Below:* Zebras live in families that often graze the plains in large herds. When attacked, a zebra family runs off together, with a stallion in the rear fending off the attacker. *Opposite:* Zebras taking a communal drink. They often share water holes and grasslands with antelopes, buffaloes, and wildebeests.

far and away the largest of any land animal alive today. Further highlighting its unmistakable identity is its elongated trunk, which forms from the nose and upper lip. This long breathing apparatus extends the elephant's reach and is used for heavy lifting, as well as delicate operations such as rubbing an eye.

The elephant's herding characteristics resemble those of the hippo's, with females and calves comprising large groups and males forming smaller ones. A female elephant giving birth is often accompanied by another female elephant, which acts as a sort of midwife during labor and babysitter after the calf is born.

Elephants show a high degree of intelligence. They are very protective of other elephants that have fallen sick or become injured. They also display a great deal of concern over dead elephants – even skeletal remains. The extraordinary luster of their ivory has created a high demand for their tusks. This exacerbates the ongoing threat to the survival of the species.

Towering above the mammoth, herbivorous elephant, the yellow and brown giraffe freely browses the savanna treetops. It feeds on the leaves of branches between seven and 18 feet from the ground – leaves clearly out of the reach of other grazing mammals.

After giving birth, a mother giraffe closely guards her young calf; initially the mother will not allow another giraffe near the calf. This unusual behavior changes after a few

Zebra herds sometimes number as many as 10,000. During the night they remain grouped together in the open grassy plains.

Below: A Nile crocodile, *Crocodylus niloticus,* basks in the sun on a river bank. Crocodiles spend much of their lives in the water and can remain submerged for up to an hour. *Opposite:* A Nile crocodile demonstrates its powerful jaws. Crocodile parents scoop up their newborn young in these terrifying mandibles and ferry them away to secluded nurseries in the swamp.

weeks, when the calf is left in a "nursery group." Entrusted to another adult female, which watches over a whole group of calves, the young giraffe eats and plays all day while its mother feeds elsewhere.

Lions, leopards, and hyenas prey on young giraffes, and only 25 to 50 percent live beyond their first year.

Big cats – lions, leopards, cheetahs – are the largest of the plains predators. Leopards and cheetahs live singly or in pairs while lions live in groups called prides.

Lion prides usually consist of 15 to 20 lions, of which three to five are adult males. It is up to them to defend their reign against other males, which occasionally attempt to make the pride their own. Males, larger and heavier than females, are easily distinguished by their thick, golden manes. The mane guards against another lion's claws during territorial disputes and symbolizes the male's dominance.

It is the female, however, that maintains the internal structure of the pride by fending off other female lions. All females in a pride are related; the males, however, leave the pride as young adults for a nomadic existence before settling down with a new pride as part of the male hierarchy.

Preceding page: **The common agama, or rainbow lizard,** *Agama agama,* **frequents the hard ground of the African savanna in abundant family groups of five to 25. A dominant male heads the family and defends it and its territory.** *This page, top to bottom:* **Male agama lizards typically display bright colors. Among Africa's poisonous snakes is the puff adder,** *Bitis arietans,* **which hisses, or puffs, loudly when irritated. When the poisonous Egyptian cobra,** *Naja haje,* **is disturbed, it will rise up and spread the skin around its neck into a threatening hood, making the snake appear larger than it really is.**

Male lions kill for food from time to time, but usually it is the females that do the hunting. Several females stalk their prey – antelopes, hartebeests, zebras – and when close enough, lunge from their grassy cover. Hunting in small groups of three to four, they work together to bring their victim down and make the kill, usually with a piercing bite to the neck. Immediately after the kill is made, the males of the pride charge the scene and chase the females away. Only after the males and cubs have had their fill do the females return to eat.

Neither the cheetah nor the leopard are social like the lion. Cheetahs live in pairs or very small groups of three to four, and the leopard leads a solitary existence. Cheetahs hunt on open plains primarily during early morning hours or in the late afternoon. Known as the world's fastest running animal, the cheetah relies heavily on its speed to overtake its prey. A gazelle, an extremely fast and maneuverable animal, will allow a lion to get relatively close to it, but a cheetah at 100 yards is too close for comfort. The cheetah's thin build and long legs explain short bursts of speed up to 75 miles per hour.

Preceding page: Marabou storks, *Leptoptilus crumeniferus,* are found only in Africa and have a diet ranging from crocodile eggs to flamingos. *This page, top to bottom:* A pair of crowned cranes, *Balearica regulorum,* sports tufts of yellow contour features, topping a beautiful mix of gray, black, white, and red feathers. The marabou stork's 12-foot wingspan places it among the world's largest birds. The shoebill stork, or whalehead, *Balaeniceps rex,* uses its huge beak to crack the shells of small turtles on which it feeds.

The sky appears a vivid pink when a flock of flamingos, *Phoeniconaias minor,* flies overhead. Their colonies sometimes number 20,000. *Below:* Not yet as beautifully pink as their parents, young flamingos feed en masse, sweeping their uniquely bent bills through the water to filter out tiny organisms.

A secretary bird, *Sagittarius secretarius*, takes to the air in Kenya. This large bird kills its prey with repetitive hammerlike blows of its bill. *Below:* Vultures primarily eat carrion, although on occasion some species kill newborn antelopes. Their closed circling signals jackals and other scavengers that a meal can be found nearby.

Preceding pages, left: Baboon parents keep a watchful eye on their infant. As baboons spend most of their time on the ground, they depend upon the group effort of their troop to avoid leopards and other large predators. *Right:* A chacma baboon, *Papio ursinus,* nurses her young in the Kruger National Park of South Africa. *This page:* Distinguished by its white collar of fur, the Syke's monkey, *Cercopithecus kolbi,* is one of the largest Old World monkeys.

Right: A family of black-faced vervets, *Cercopithecus aethiops,* will soon share the fruit of this large nut. *Below:* Vervet monkeys spend most of their time in trees. Their very long tails increase their ability to balance, but are not prehensile.

The leopard is stockier than the cheetah and uses power rather than speed to make a kill; a 20-foot, horizontal leap testifies to the cat's strong hind legs. Of the African cats, the leopard is the most adept in trees: It spends much of its day lying on a limb and will often drag a freshly killed animal onto the fork of a tree branch for safekeeping. Away from scavengers, a large animal such as an antelope will provide food for the leopard for two or three nights. Leopards have adapted to a nocturnal life and live in solitude, pairing only to mate. The trees and dense brush of their habitat make it unnecessary to hunt in groups.

Caracals and servals are smaller cats which feed primarily on rodents and birds. The serval is slightly larger than the caracal and can be found stalking in areas of taller grass. The caracal frequents streams and woodland areas where it hunts at night.

Cats, big and small, are the most effective hunters on the African plains. Their speed, strength, agility, and razor-sharp claws make anything fair game.

Hyenas, wild dogs, and jackals act as both predators and scavengers. These animals represent the canine, or dog order.

Jackals hunt alone or in pairs. They have a varied diet but rarely kill animals larger than birds or rodents; they will occasionally eat remnants of a lion kill.

Wild dogs are strictly social. They hunt in packs of 10 to 15 and depend upon team effort to bring down a large mammal such as a gazelle or even a zebra.

The baobab tree is the only large tree truly adapted to life on the savanna. Its fibrous wood retains enough water to last a long dry season. Elephants chew its spongy wood to extract juices.

Left: The hippopotamus, *Hippopotamus amphibius,* spends most of the day just floating in rivers or lakes. It comes ashore to feed during the night. *Below:* Three hippos meander along the headwaters of the Nile River in Uganda. Docile only in appearance, hippopotamuses rarely back away from other animals and can be quite dangerous.

Above: Hippos can stay submerged in water for up to six minutes. Females live in herds; smaller male groups inhabit inland mud wallows.

Preceding page: Poor eyesight and a willingness to charge any suspected enemy have led to a reputation of ill temperament for the rhinoceros, *Diceros bicornis.* This black rhino stands alert, ready to charge. *This page:* The white rhinoceros, *Ceratotherium simum,* typically feeds on grass during daylight hours. Tick birds help keep the rhino free of parasitic and biting insects.

Hyenas hunt as individuals and also in packs. During daylight, when a lone hyena is on the prowl as a scavenger, it occasionally hunts gazelles. During the dark of the night, hyenas form packs and easily kill very large grazers such as the wildebeest.

Aardwolves, mongooses, genets, civets, and foxes are also carnivores of the African plains. Their diets vary, but collectively they consume insects, small rodents, birds, eggs, and reptiles.

One should not be surprised that the ostrich, the world's largest bird, would be found in Africa, land of extremes. Wandering the grasslands in flocks of 12 to 50 birds, the ostrich stands lookout not only for itself, but often for zebras and other grazers, which respond to the bird's cues. In return for this security, the zebras provide food to the big birds by scaring up snakes and lizards.

Ostriches are among the few birds of the world that cannot fly. Instead, they run extremely fast; capable of outrunning a charging lion, ostriches have reached speeds of up to 30 miles per hour.

An ostrich lays 10 to 12 eggs at a time. The largest eggs in the world, ostrich eggs measure up to nine inches in length, six inches across,

Crossing the plains beneath a setting sun, these giraffes, *Giraffa camelopardalis*, create a purely African image. Perfectly suited to the savanna, giraffes need hard ground for support, as they can weigh more than a ton and their small feet would quickly sink into loose dirt. *Following pages, left:* Only after several weeks will a mother giraffe entrust her young to a group nursery. Such cooperative effort allows mothers enough time to browse for the large quantity of leaves needed to sustain such a heavy animal. *Right:* A giraffe browses the top of a thorny acacia tree. Frequent episodes with stinging ants keep giraffes moving from tree to tree.

and have a shell one-quarter-inch thick. This size makes the egg a tempting meal to several predators like the jackal, hyena, and the Egyptian vulture, which breaks the hard shell by hitting it with a stone and then consumes its contents. A parenting ostrich will often leave the nest and feign a broken wing in order to draw predators away from the eggs.

As birds generally migrate lengthy distances, most species emerge on several different continents. Pelicans and flamingos happen to be native to the marshes of the African plains. When feeding, pelicans skim the water surface and adroitly scoop up fish; flamingos filter algae from the water or snag shrimp from the muddy bottom; marabou storks, in turn, kill and eat flamingos.

The vast population of flamingos is kept in check by the marabou, a bird which is *only* found in Africa. During the nesting season, marabou storks invade the nesting area of flamingos and consume quantities of chicks. They also attack flocks of adult flamingos feeding in the water. As the stork approaches the flock, the flamingos flee very haphazardly, making it quite easy for a stork to trap one. Marabous have a varied diet: They also feed on dead fish, crocodile eggs, and meat stolen from vultures dissecting a carcass.

Matriarch-dominated elephant groups herd together when food and water become scarce. Smaller bands of bull elephants normally travel in the same direction. *Overleaf:* Looking like statues, these young African elephants, *Loxodonta africana,* have covered themselves with mud to protect against the heat of the sun and biting insects. Mudwallowing is common behavior for Africa's largest mammals.

Various amphibians and reptiles easily find their niche on the African plains. The rivers and marshes of the plains are well suited for snakes, frogs, and crocodiles because of the ever-warming sun and an abundance of insects and small rodents.

Crocodiles frequent the habitat of hippopotamuses and occasionally kill small hippo calves left unprotected, although they usually feed on large fish, birds, and smaller mammals. They have a slow metabolism and often need only one big meal for an entire week. Crocodiles, which basically live in the water, can remain submerged for up to an hour. As with too many of the animals on the African plains, the future of crocodiles looks bleak due to poaching and destruction of their habitat.

As the rainy season draws to a close, the animals' behavior and the land begin to change. The elephant will not wander as far from known water holes and wildebeests form large herds to search for better grazing areas. Plants turn from green to brown; the ground begins to crack. And paradise reverts to its better-known self – the hot, dry, gray stretch of land called the African plains.

Looming large against the blue sky of Tanzania, this African elephant displays a perfect pair of ivory tusks. An individual's tusks rarely look exactly alike. Elephants tend to be right- or left- "handed," causing more wear to one tusk than the other.

Index of Photography

TIB indicates The Image Bank

DATE DUE